COLOR YOUR OWN
Van Gogh Paintings

Vincent van Gogh

Rendered by Marty Noble

DOVER PUBLICATIONS, INC.
Mineola, New York

NOTE

Expressive brushwork, the heightened use of color, and an intense emotionality epitomize the individualized style of Vincent van Gogh (1853–1890). The oldest child of a pastor, the Dutch Post-Impressionist tried such varied careers as language teacher, art dealer, and preacher before he began to paint in earnest in 1880. During the first four years of his painting, he specialized in drawings and watercolors. From 1884 until his premature death, the destitute van Gogh focused his talents on oil painting.

Inspired by Impressionism, Japanese prints, and French painting, van Gogh soon developed a unique style. He attempted to organize a working artists' community in Arles with Toulouse-Lautrec and Gauguin, but a quarrel with Gauguin in 1888 provoked van Gogh into cutting off part of his own ear. Plagued through-out his life with mental difficulties, van Gogh was admitted to an asylum at his own request.

Van Gogh's artistic career was brief, lasting merely one decade. Distraught and riddled with despair, he took his own life in 1890. Sadly, it was only after his death that popular attention was drawn to his work. Although he sold just one painting during his lifetime, van Gogh produced 800 oil paintings and 700 drawings.

Rendered by artist Marty Noble, the thirty van Gogh paintings in this book will appeal to any-one interested in fine art. All of the paintings in this collection are featured in full color on the inside front and back covers. Use this color scheme as a guide to create your own adaptation of a van Gogh or change the colors to see the effects of color and tone on each painting. Captions identify the title of the work, date of composition, and the medium employed.

Bibliographical Note

Color Your Own van Gogh Paintings is a new work, first published by Dover Publications, Inc., in 1999.

DOVER *Pictorial Archive* SERIES

This book belongs to the Dover Pictorial Archive Series. You may use the designs and illustrations for graphics and crafts applications, free and without special permission, provided that you include no more than four in the same publication or project. (For permission for additional use, please write to Permissions Department, Dover Publications, Inc., 31 East 2nd Street, Mineola, N.Y. 11501.)

However, republication or reproduction of any illustration by any other graphic service, whether it be in a book or in any other design resource, is strictly prohibited.

International Standard Book Number: 0-486-40570-2

Manufactured in the United States of America
Dover Publications, Inc., 31 East 2nd Street, Mineola, N.Y. 11501

1. **Portrait of the Postman Joseph Roulin.** 1888. Oil on canvas.

2.   **La Berceuse (Augustine Roulin).** 1889. Oil on canvas.

3. **L'Arlésienne: Madame Ginoux with Books.** 1888 or 1889. Oil on canvas.

4. **Still Life: Vase with Irises.** 1890. Oil on canvas.

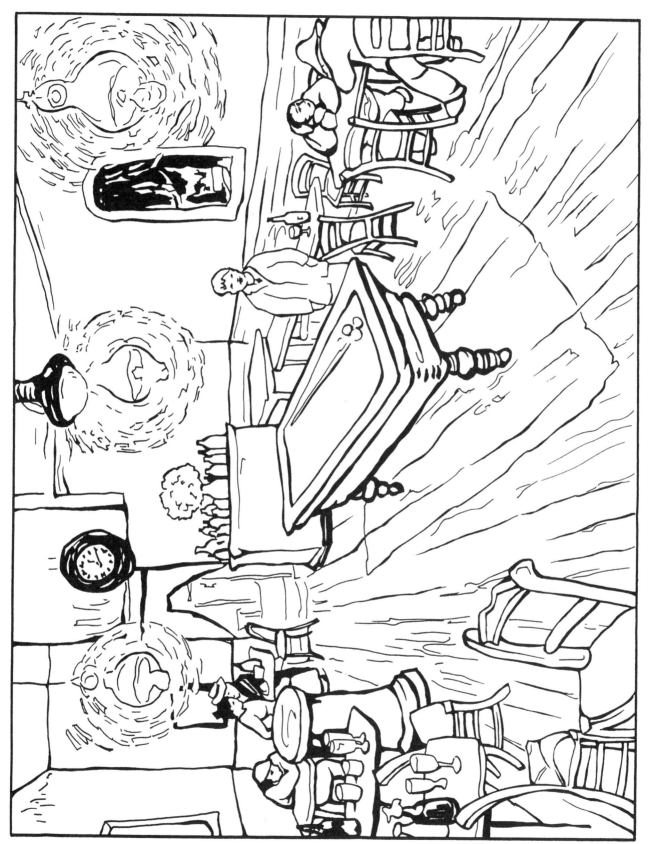

5. The Night Café in the Place Lamartine in Arles. 1888. Oil on canvas.

6. Van Gogh's Bedroom. 1888. Oil on canvas.

7. Olive Trees. 1889. Oil on canvas.

8. **Still Life: Vase with Twelve Sunflowers.** 1888. Oil on canvas.

9. **Young Peasant Woman with Straw Hat Sitting in the Wheat.** 1890. Oil on canvas.

10. **Street in Saintes-Maries**. 1888. Oil on canvas.

11.   **The Road Menders.** 1889. Oil on canvas.

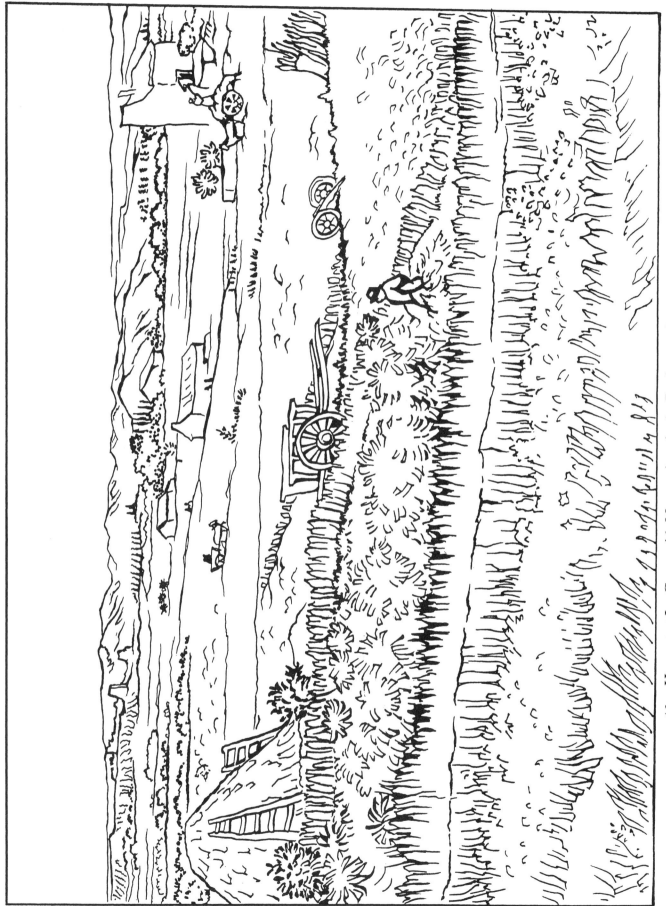

12.   Harvest at La Crau, with Montmajour in the Background. 1888. Oil on canvas.

13. The Langlois Bridge at Arles with Women Washing. 1888. Oil on canvas.

14. **Noon Rest** (After Millet). 1890. Oil on canvas.

15. **Starry Night**. 1889. Oil on canvas.

16.   **Portrait of Patience Escalier.** 1888. Oil on canvas.

17.   **La Mousmé, Seated in a Cane Chair.** 1888. Oil on canvas.

18. **Old Man in Sorrow (On the Threshold of Eternity).** 1890. Oil on canvas.

19.   **Portrait of Doctor Gachet.** 1890. Oil on canvas.

20.   **Self-Portrait with Bandaged Ear and Pipe.** 1889. Oil on canvas.

21. **Vincent's Chair with His Pipe.** 1888. Oil on canvas.

22.   **Two Little Girls.** 1890. Oil on canvas.

23. **Portrait of Père Tanguy.** 1887. Oil on canvas.

24. Vincent's House in Arles (The Yellow House). 1888. Oil on canvas.

25. Fishing Boats on the Beach at Saintes-Maries. 1888. Oil on canvas.

26. **The Church at Auvers.** 1890. Oil on canvas.

27. **Self-Portrait.** 1889. Oil on canvas.

28. **Café Terrace at Night.** 1888. Oil on canvas.

29. **Entrance to the Asylum.** 1889. Gouache.

30. Village Street in Auvers. 1890. Oil on canvas.